Hampstead Middle School

796.32 MAH
Mahaney, Ian F.   The math of basketball

P9-CBB-131

DATE DUE

JUN 1 5 2022	

HAMPSTEAD MIDDLE SCHOOL
MEDIA CENTER

The Math of
Basketball

Ian F. Mahaney

PowerKiDS press™

New York

For Brenda

Published in 2012 by The Rosen Publishing Group, Inc.
29 East 21st Street, New York, NY 10010

Copyright © 2012 by The Rosen Publishing Group, Inc.

All rights reserved. No part of this book may be reproduced in any form without permission in writing from the publisher, except by a reviewer.

First Edition

Editor: Joanne Randolph
Layout Design: Greg Tucker

Photo Credits: Cover, pp. 10–11 (main), 16–17 Christian Peterson/Getty Images; pp. 4–5 Doug Pensinger/ Getty Images; pp. 6 (inset), 7 (inset), 8 (inset), 11 (inset) Shutterstock.com; pp. 6–7 (main) Brian Babineau/NBAE/Getty Images; pp. 8–9 (main) Noah Graham/Getty Images; pp. 12–13 Otto Greule Jr./ Getty Images; p. 14 (inset) Jamie Squire/Getty Images; pp. 14–15 (main), 18–19 Jonathan Daniel/Getty Images; pp. 20–21 Brian Bahr/Getty Images.

Library of Congress Cataloging-in-Publication Data

Mahaney, Ian F.
 The math of basketball / by Ian F. Mahaney. — 1st ed.
     p. cm. — (Sports math)
 Includes index.
 ISBN 978-1-4488-2593-6 (library binding) — ISBN 978-1-4488-2694-0 (pbk.) —
 ISBN 978-1-4488-2695-7 (6-pack)
 1. Basketball—Mathematics—Juvenile literature. I. Title.
 GV885.1.M35 2012
 796.3230151—dc22
                              2010027917

Manufactured in the United States of America

CPSIA Compliance Information: Batch #WW11PK: For Further Information contact Rosen Publishing, New York, New York at 1-800-237-9932

Contents

How Does Basketball Work?

In basketball, two teams play on a court that has baskets on either end. Each team is allowed five players on the court. The remaining players sit on the side waiting to play. Each team gets points when players put the basketball into the team's basket. The team that scores the most points wins the game.

Players wear uniforms to make it easy to tell which team they are on.

The team with the ball is called the **offense**. It is trying to score. The other team is the **defense** and tries to stop the offense from scoring.

Basketball is full of math. Your math skills can help you learn more about this fast-paced game.

Figure It Out!

The Denver Nuggets have nine players in uniform for a game and five are playing on the court. How many players are waiting to play on the bench?

(See page 22 for the answers.)

A basketball court is shaped like a rectangle. The National Basketball Association (NBA) is a **professional league**. An NBA court is 94 feet (29 m) long and 50 feet (15 m) wide. The court is divided in half and each team defends one half. Do you want to figure out how

This picture shows what a basketball court looks like. The small circles with the lines behind them are the baskets.

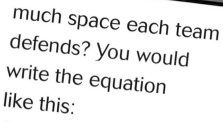

much space each team defends? You would write the equation like this:

94 feet ÷ 2 = 47 feet. To find the area of one half of the court, you would then write:

47 feet x 50 feet = 2,350 square feet.

The two baskets are on either end of the court, along the short sides of the rectangle. The baskets are 10 feet (3 m) off the ground and measure 18 inches (46 cm) wide.

Here the player in maroon is trying to defend the basket from the offensive player in white.

The ball's **diameter** is about 9 inches (23 cm). How much smaller is the basketball than the basket?

(See page 22 for the answers.)

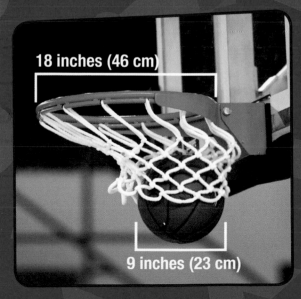

18 inches (46 cm)

9 inches (23 cm)

Point Math

The object of most games is to score more points than the other team. This is true in basketball as well. When a player makes a basket, it is generally worth two points. However, when a player makes

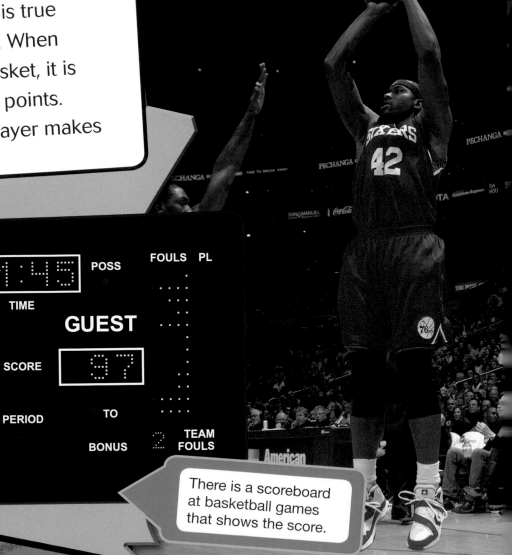

PL	FOULS	POSS	01:45	POSS	FOULS	PL
			TIME			
		HOME		GUEST		
		103	SCORE	97		
		TO	PERIOD	TO		
TEAM FOULS	6	BONUS		BONUS	2	TEAM FOULS

There is a scoreboard at basketball games that shows the score.

a basket past a certain line on the court, it is worth three points. That line is called the three-point line. It lets the players know how far away they need to be to score three points. In the NBA, the three-point line is between 22 feet (6.7 m) and 23 feet 9 inches (7.2 m) from the basket. Some leagues do not have three-point lines.

This player is taking a two-point shot. You can see the three-point line behind him.

Figure It Out!

A person can do some quick math to find out how far behind one team is from the other. Say the Denver Nuggets are losing to the Utah Jazz 92–84. How many points behind are the Nuggets? What is the fewest number of baskets they can make to take the lead?

(See page 22 for the answers.)

Fouls

The defense tries to do everything it can to stop the offense from scoring. This includes guarding the offensive players, or trying to keep them from getting passes or making shots.

In order to make the game fair, the defense has to follow certain rules when trying to stop the other team. The defense cannot push,

It's a Fact!

The offense can be charged with a foul, too. An offensive player cannot run over a defensive player when the defensive player is standing still. This is called a charge. When it happens, a foul is called. The other team gets the ball.

hit, hold on to, or run into an offensive player. If a defensive player breaks these rules, he gets a foul. Sometimes the offensive player receives free throws when he is fouled. A free throw is a chance to score while the person shooting is not defended. The players take free throws from the free-throw line. Each free throw made is worth one point.

Figure It Out!

During a basketball game, free throws can add many points to a team's score. If the Los Angeles Sparks, a women's professional basketball team, score 4 three-point shots, 32 two-points shots, and 13 free throws, how many points have they scored?

(See page 22 for the answers.)

Here Tony Allen of the Boston Celtics is fouling Kobe Bryant of the Los Angeles Lakers.

Candace Parker plays for the Los Angeles Sparks. She makes about 70 percent of the free throws she takes.

Free-Throw Percentages

Free throws are a great chance to score. Players that make the most of free throws add many points to their teams' score. Coaches and fans pay close attention to how often each player makes free throws instead of missing.

A free-throw percentage shows how often a player makes free throws. It is found by dividing the

Karl Malone of the Utah Jazz has a career free-throw percentage of .742. He made the most free throws in the league for seven seasons, an NBA record.

number of free throws made by the number of attempts. If John has five free-throw attempts and makes three of them, his free-throw percentage is $3 \div 5 = 0.600$. That means John makes 60 percent of his free throws. Free-throw percentages are generally rounded to three decimal places.

If a player gets 15 free throws and makes 4 of them, what is her free-throw percentage?
A) $15 + 4 = 19\%$
B) $15 \div 4 = 3.750$
C) $4 \div 15 = 0.266$

(See page 22 for the answers.)

Time

The length of basketball games depends on the league. NBA games are 48 minutes long. Their games are split into four equal time segments, called quarters. To find out how long each quarter is, you can do some math:

48 minutes ÷ 4 quarters = 12 minutes.

There is a clock on the court that tells the time left in the quarter. The red number beneath that time is the shot clock, which gives a team 24 seconds to shoot the ball.

In the National Collegiate Athletic Association (NCAA), the biggest collegiate basketball league, the game length is 40 minutes. This time is split into two equal periods, called halves. If you divide 40 by 2, you will find that each half is 20 minutes long.

Between the two halves or between the second and third quarters, there is a break called halftime. The players and coaches rest and **strategize** during halftime.

College games, like this one between the West Virginia University Mountaineers and the Duke University Blue Devils, are shorter than NBA games.

Figure It Out!

High-school basketball games are often 32 minutes long, played in four quarters. How long do the quarters last?
A) $32 \times 4 = 128$ minutes
B) $32 \div 4 = 8$ minutes
C) $32 + 4 = 36$ minutes

(See page 22 for the answers.)

HAMPSTEAD MIDDLE SCHOOL
MEDIA CENTER

The Play-offs

In the NBA, the regular season is 82 games long. The best 16 teams **qualify** for the **play-offs**.

The play-offs are a **tournament**. Teams are **eliminated** from the play-offs when they lose **series**. In the first round of the play-offs, 16 teams play in eight series of games. Each series is made up of seven games. A team needs to win four games in its series to move on to the next round. To find out how many teams in the first round will move on, you would write:

$16 \div 2 = 8.$

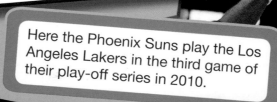
Here the Phoenix Suns play the Los Angeles Lakers in the third game of their play-off series in 2010.

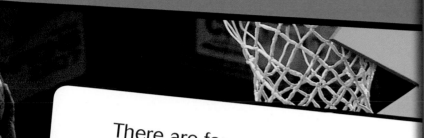

Figure It Out!

There are four rounds in the play-offs. In each round, half the teams are eliminated. In the last round, called the NBA Finals, there are only two teams left. The winner is the champion of the league.

A basketball league has a tournament like the NBA's play-offs. In these play-offs, there are 32 teams in the first round. How many teams will be left after the second round is played?

(See page 22 for the answers.)

Dare to Compare

Statistics, or stats, is the study and understanding of groups of numbers. Fans, coaches, and players can compare the stats of different players and teams to **evaluate** which ones are better.

Michael Jordan	2002–03 Highs	Career Highs
Points	45	69
Field goals made	18	27
Field goals attempted	33	49
Three-point field goals made	3	7
Three-point field goals attempted	4	12
Free throws made	13	26
Free throws attempted	16	27
Offensive rebounds	5	8
Defensive rebounds	13	14
Total rebounds	14	18
Assists	12	17
Steals	6	10
Blocks	3	6
Minutes played	53	56

The most basic statistics count things related to one or more basketball games. The number of fouls a player gets is an example of a counting statistic.

More advanced statistics look at the percentage of time a player is successful at something. An example is field-goal percentage (FG%). A field goal is a successful two- or three-point basket. To find a player's FG%, divide the number of successful field goals by the number of attempts.

Figure It Out!

Michael Jordan is known as one of the NBA's greatest players. During his career, he made 12,192 field goals in 24,537 attempts. What was his career field-goal percentage? You might need a calculator for this one!

(See page 22 for the answers.)

Michael Jordan scored 32,292 points in his career playing basketball!

Top Teams

Statistics are important for teams, too. In order to win games, teams need to make a high percentage of their free throws and keep the number of fouls they get low.

The most important statistic for teams is winning percentage. Having a great winning percentage helps a team qualify for the play-offs. In the 1995–1996 NBA season, the Chicago Bulls won 72 games and lost 10 games. To find their winning percentage, we divide the games played from those they won: $72 \div (72 + 10) = 0.878$. That means they won nearly 90 percent of their games! With this stat, the Bulls had the best winning percentage in NBA history. They qualified for the play-offs and won the NBA championship that year, too.

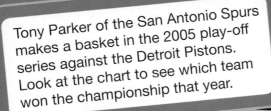

Tony Parker of the San Antonio Spurs makes a basket in the 2005 play-off series against the Detroit Pistons. Look at the chart to see which team won the championship that year.

Figure It Out!

This chart shows which teams had the best winning percentage and which team won the championship. How many teams with the best winning percentage won the championship? What percentage of teams with the best winning percentage goes on to win the championship? Are you surprised?

Year	Best Winning %	NBA Champ
2000–2001	San Antonio Spurs	LA Lakers
2001–2002	Sacramento Kings	LA Lakers
2002–2003	San Antonio Spurs	San Antonio Spurs
2003–2004	Indiana Pacers	Detroit Pistons
2004–2005	Phoenix Suns	San Antonio Spurs
2005–2006	Detroit Pistons	Miami Heat
2006–2007	Dallas Mavericks	San Antonio Spurs
2007–2008	Boston Celtics	Boston Celtics
2008–2009	Cleveland Cavaliers	LA Lakers
2009-2010	Cleveland Cavaliers	LA Lakers

(See page 22 for the answers.)

Figure It Out: The Answers

Page 5: There are 9 − 5 = 4 players on the bench.

Page 7: The basketball is 18 inches − 9 inches = 9 inches smaller than the basket.

Page 9: The Nuggets are behind by 8 points (92 − 84 = 8). The Nuggets need 9 points to take the lead, or three 3-point baskets: 84 + 3 + 3 + 3 = 93 points or 84 + 3 x 3 = 93.

Page 11: The Sparks have (4 x 3) + (32 x 2) + (13 x 1) = 12 + 64 + 13 = 89 points.

Page 13: C) "Percent" means "parts per 100." To convert a decimal (0.266) to a percent, multiply the decimal by 100. 0.266 x 100 = 26.6%. This player needs to practice her free throws!

Page 15: B)

Page 17: Eight teams are left after the second round (16 ÷ 2 = 8). To find this answer, you first have to know how many teams were left after the first round, which was 16 teams (32 ÷ 2 = 16).

Page 19: 12,192 ÷ 24,537 = 0.497. That is 49.7%.

Page 21: Two teams, San Antonio in 2002–2003 and Boston in 2007–2008, had the best winning percentage and won the NBA Finals. The percent that did this is 2 ÷ 10 = 20%.

Glossary

defense (DEE-fents) The team that tries to stop the other team from scoring.

diameter (dy-A-meh-ter) The measurement across the center of a round object.

eliminated (ih-LIH-muh-nayt-ed) Removed.

evaluate (ih-VAL-yuh-wayt) To think about the importance of something.

league (LEEG) A group of teams that play one another.

offense (uh-fents) The team trying to score points.

play-offs (PLAY-ofs) Games played after the regular season ends to see who will play in the championship game.

professional (pruh-FESH-nul) Someone who is paid for what he or she does.

qualify (KWAH-lih-fy) To meet the requirements of something.

series (SIR-eez) A group of games played one after another, generally on different days.

strategize (STRA-teh-jyz) To plan different plays in team sports.

tournament (TOR-nuh-ment) A group of games to decide the best player or team.

Index

Web Sites

Due to the changing nature of Internet links, PowerKids Press has developed an online list of Web sites related to the subject of this book. This site is updated regularly. Please use this link to access the list:
www.powerkidslinks.com/sm/basket/